FOUND *in* EMPTINESS

Rhonda L. Kendall

ISBN: 978-1-4834-7163-1 (sc)
ISBN: 978-1-4834-7162-4 (e)

Library of Congress Control Number: 2017909920

Lulu Publishing Services rev. date: 06/28/2017

And the earth was without form, and void; and darkness was upon the face of the deep. And the Spirit of God moved upon the face of the waters.

—Genesis 1:2 KJV

CONTENTS

ACKNOWLEDGMENTS

Thanks be unto God from whom all blessings flow. It was His grace that provided me with the strength to finish the work birthed from pain and disappointment yet delivered by purpose and with praise.

To you—my love, my rock, my confidant, my loyal friend, and my life partner. I have become the best me because God gave me you. Thank you for facing every trial with me head-on—sometimes beside me, while other times carrying me. Robert Kendall III, I love you.

And to my mom, there aren't enough words to convey the immeasurable gratitude I have for all you have done for me. I thank God for choosing you just for me.

Last, but not least —Lana Marie, your mommy loved you before you were ever conceived. This work is dedicated to you so you will know that *nothing* is impossible with God.

Introduction

EMPTINESS

Emptiness. A commonly used synonym for this word is "void." This is where nothing can be found, nor can anything be contained. You can't find your peace—it now eludes you. You can't find joy—it has escaped from your very grasp. You can't hold on any longer, and it feels like even God Himself has left you. Many of us have found ourselves here by happenstance due to situations beyond our control. What occurred may not have been fair, and it did not give us an opportunity to prepare ourselves for what seems like an eternal stay in the empty place. This place does not offer the amenities of comfort or hope. Instead it's dark, and although there are many here at the same place and time—it's still lonely.

"Eli, Eli, lama sabachthani?" These words, translated, "*My God, my God, why hast thou forsaken me?*" were cried by Jesus at about the ninth hour while hanging on the cross at Calvary (Matthew 27:46 KJV). As I mourned the loss of my son and daughter, buried on Christmas Eve 2014, these words rang out in my spirit: "Eli, Eli, lama sabachthani?" Through tears, I spoke to God in my heart from an empty place, wondering why He had forsaken me.

With these words in mind, I write this book for all of those who, like me, are searching for God in an empty place. The Word of God says in Matthew 28:20b, "Lo, I am with you always, even unto the end of the world. Amen" (KJV). Knowing this, we ask ourselves, how do we find God within the vast void left by a devastating loss, a broken marriage, a shattered dream, or even our own failures?

Chapter 1

ON THE ENEMY'S PLAYGROUND

"Why is God punishing me?"

"What did I do to deserve this?"

"Why me?"

If we are honest, all of us have asked at least one of these questions at some point in our lives, whether we have a relationship with God or not. Whether you are saved, sanctified, and filled with the Holy Ghost or haven't found yourself in a church in years, somehow one of or all of these questions have crossed your mind. Some of you may feel guilty for even contemplating these questions because you were taught to never question God. Others simply come from a place of anguish and despair. These questions and feelings are a common response to a devastating situation, and you feel God is nowhere to be found. Take heart! You are not alone in these feelings. Be encouraged—God knows the sincerity of your heart and the depth of your pain. There isn't a feeling you have felt or a thought you have had that God was not aware of before it came to be—and He still loves you.

The Bible says in Hebrews 4:15 (NIV), "For we do not have a high priest who is unable to empathize with our weaknesses, but we have one who has been tempted in every way, just as we are—yet he did not sin." Simply speaking, Christ is able to empathize (to have the *same* feelings as another person) with what you are going through. How? Because He chose to enter our world to walk in our skin and feel what we feel so He can give us hope! The human man who died at Calvary for us felt physical and emotional pain, sorrow, and grief, and He experienced loss. Understand that the Bible may not specify how Christ endured your specific situation, but it does show at some point that He felt the emotion invoked by your situation. So if He cares, why did He allow this to happen? Good question. Keep reading, and I pray God will enlighten you along the way.

In the midst of despair, it is not uncommon to be tempted to concede the fight or give up on ministry. You may be ready to give up on your children, throw away your career, or end your marriage—or maybe even your life! These temptations come when you're in an empty place. The void that has been left by this hurt you feel is seemingly unbearable. Before you make a permanent decision for a temporary situation, I need you to recognize that there is also someone else beside you in your empty place—and that is the devil. The scriptures say, "Be sober, be vigilant; because your adversary the devil, as a roaring lion, walketh about, seeking whom he may devour" (1 Peter 5:8 KJV). To be vigilant means to be keenly watchful to detect danger. Simply put: *pay attention—danger, danger!* The empty place is the devil's hunting ground, and he is on the prowl. He will use your very feelings against you to plant seeds of anger, hatred, bitterness, and depression.

Your pain is the soil he will use to cultivate these seeds until they grow into strongholds.

Spiritual strongholds become negative and harmful habits, beliefs, or behaviors built in the mind that are not easily broken. To put it plainly, a stronghold is equivalent to *mental prison*. Once a person is physically imprisoned in a jail cell, there is only one way out—and only an authorized prison official can open those bars. It is the same when you are mentally confined by illegal thoughts and mind-sets. Yes—*illegal*. These thoughts and mind-sets are trespassing on territory that does not belong to them. The Bible says in 2 Timothy 1:7 (AMP), "For God did not give us a spirit of timidity or cowardice or fear, but [He has given us a spirit] of power and of love and of sound judgment and personal discipline [abilities that result in a calm, well-balanced mind and self-control]."

We must keep watch as we process our pain, for the Word of God says in 2 Corinthians 2:11 (NLT), "So that Satan will not outsmart us. For we are familiar with his evil schemes." Contrary to what the devil wants you to believe, the authority for your release has already been given to you by the Holy Spirit. The power to fight back against the negative seeds planted and against the strongholds that come to imprison you is in your mouth! During this time, I urge you to reflect on the thoughts that come into your mind. Verbally cast down (push out of your mind) any of those thoughts that are contrary to the truth that you know has been revealed in times past by the Holy Spirit. Begin to speak out of your mouth the words that will change the atmosphere that surrounds you. Tell yourself (and the devil) the opposite of what you feel. You may feel like giving up—but say aloud, "I will not give up!" You may feel like dying—but say aloud, "I will live and not die!" Most important, bring those thoughts and feelings to God, and lay them at His feet in prayer. This is where you will find spiritual strength to declare these words. As I stated, He already knows. He is waiting for us to confess them to Him. "Casting all your care upon him; for he careth for you" (1 Peter 5:7 KJV).

While you are in this place, the enemy will do his best to make you feel as if you are not a "strong enough

Christian" because you hurt in a way contrary to popular belief. He will use people to make you feel as if you've grieved for too long or you didn't have enough faith to see the manifestation of your prayer request. They may even make you feel like you've backslid or are paying for your own sins. I challenge you to turn a deaf ear to those he sends to discourage you. Instead, look to Jesus as your example:

1. In Luke 22:42 (KJV), Jesus says, "Saying, Father, if thou be willing, remove this cup from me: nevertheless not my will, but thine, be done." Many people place emphasis on the latter part of that scripture—the "nevertheless." We should all have this response to God's will. However, take note that even Jesus asked the Father to "remove this cup from me." His suffering had been great, and at one point it was more than He desired to bear. I believe those words were not uttered from within the deity of the Messiah but instead from the human emotions of the one who walked

in flesh as a man. The human Jesus too found Himself crying for relief from what He had—and still had—to endure.

2. As referenced in chapter 1, Jesus also cried to the Father while on the cross and asked God why He had forsaken Him. He understood what was transpiring and knew the truth about what had to occur; however, He did not neglect to lend voice to the feelings associated with what He had to deal with.

Do not allow people to associate *your* reaction to *your* pain with *their* idea of how you should respond. Any two people can be cut with the same knife, and yet the wounds heal at different rates. Why? Because we are all created differently, and the "knife" may cut deeper in some than others. Don't compare yourself with others—instead look to Christ. Even the Savior felt pain and cried out to the Father from the depth of those emotions as a man. Being saved does not negate our human response.

Chapter 2

BEING SAVED DOES NOT NEGATE HUMAN RESPONSES

Having a spiritual relationship with God does not mean we will not respond to hurt like any other human being. Many people who mean well may try to counsel you from solely a spiritual perspective, yet these people may never acknowledge the human, natural feelings that have come over you in waves. This can lead you to feeling as if you have lost your connection with God. You begin to doubt your relationship with God because if you were "a stronger Christian," you wouldn't have gotten angry. Instead, you would have simply acquiesced to the will of God. You must acknowledge those feelings, and after you have done so, do as Jesus did and tell God, "Nevertheless not my will, but thine, be done" (Luke 22:42b KJV).

Many studies have said there are at least five stages of grief:

1. Denial: This is when one attempts to shut out the reality or the magnitude of the situation.
2. Anger: When one realizes that one must face the situation, feelings of anger surface. This anger may be directed at others in attempt to place blame; it may be directed at God or even misdirected toward those closest. This is when questions such as, "Why me?" or such statements as, "It's not fair!" are most commonly heard.
3. Bargaining: When one hopes to find a way to undo or avoid the situation by attempting to negotiate with others (such as doctors) or even God—if only they could change what has taken place.
4. Depression: The idea of daily life or even of living in general becomes pointless. This is marked by

a change in demeanor—becoming silent, refusing visitors, and spending much time despondent and sullen. This brings about a disconnection from objects of love and affection. In this stage, there are natural feelings of sadness, regret, fear, and uncertainty, and feeling these things shows how one has begun to accept the situation.

5. Acceptance: In this final stage, one begins to come to terms with what has occurred. This typically comes with a calm, retrospective view and a stable mind-set.

We may not experience every stage. We may not experience them in that order, and the time spent in each stage may vary from person to person. The intensity of these feelings may vary in degrees by stage and by situation. We, as Christians, must learn to acknowledge these feelings rather than allow others and the enemy to condemn us because of the process. Healing is a process in and of itself, and it can never begin if we don't first recognize where we are, and accept that it is natural to *feel.*

In that empty place, the same God who created us, shaped us, and formed us in His own image also understands the process in which we grieve. In that process, and in every stage, there is a measure of grace He extends to us to see us through.

The apostle Paul, one of the Bible's greatest-known apostles, provides us with an extraordinary example of finding God in the midst of suffering. Paul opens up in 2 Corinthians 12 by speaking to the Corinthian church concerning a vision he received from the Lord. He went on to tell them that although he could, he chose not to boast of this and other revelations received from God. Rather, Paul continued his explanation by stating that in addition to the many revelations he was privileged to have had, God had also allowed Paul to suffer with "a thorn in the flesh" (the NLT *Life Application Study Bible* notes this could have possibly referred to a chronic and debilitating problem such as malaria, epilepsy, or a disease of the eyes) to keep him from becoming proud and also allowing others to exalt himself above measure. The scripture reads in verses 8–10 (AMP):

> Three times I called upon the Lord *and* besought [Him] about this *and* begged that it might depart from me; But He said to me, My grace (My favor and loving-kindness and mercy) is enough for you [sufficient against any danger and enables you to bear the trouble manfully]; for *My* strength *and* power are made perfect (fulfilled and completed) *and show themselves most effective* in [your] weakness. Therefore, I will all the more gladly glory in my weaknesses *and* infirmities, that the strength *and* power of Christ (the Messiah) may rest (yes, may pitch a tent over and dwell) upon me! So for the sake of Christ, I am well pleased *and* take pleasure in infirmities, insults, hardships, persecutions, perplexities *and* distresses;

> for when I am weak [in human strength],
> then am I [truly] strong (able, powerful in
> divine strength).

My good friend and business partner asked me sometime after the death of my twins, "How is your faith?" My answer was, "It's not my faith *in* God that is getting me through because if truth be told, this devastation has rocked it a little. But it is because there *is* a God in heaven; His *grace* is seeing me through." I learned in that moment that our unwavering faith is not what carries us—it's God's unwavering grace.

Chapter 3

CRY... SCREAM... REPEAT

Right now it's quiet. It wasn't like that a little while ago. One minute the TV is on and you're watching a semi-interesting program. The next minute you feel tightening in your chest, and you try to choke back the tears. First they begin to flow silently, just out of the corner of your eyes. Then you begin shaking your leg and tapping the top of your thigh. Then it comes out—the loud cries that you had held back ... and then the screaming. You let it all out until your head hurts, your nose is stuffed up, and your eyes are bloodshot. Then you compose yourself—until the cycle repeats.

Tears are what come from the faucet housing your hurt. You cannot control what turns that faucet on and off. It could be a memory, a song, or something you see. That is why this cycle remains on repeat, and that is okay. God knows all about what you are going through, so much so that the scripture says, "You keep track of all my sorrows. You have collected all my tears in your bottle. You have recorded each one in your book" (Psalm 56:8 NLT).

Even Jesus wept (John 11:35). The reason He cried may be different from the reason you cry. However, the fact remains that something pricked His heart and it caused Him to weep. Do not allow others to dictate how long you grieve or how many tears are enough. Instead, allow the Holy Spirit to be at work in you, fulfilling His assignment as your Comforter. The scripture does not allude that the Holy Spirit will take away the pain, yet rather He comforts you as you endure the pain. "And I will pray the Father, and he shall give you another Comforter, that he may abide with you for ever" (John 14:16 KJV).

At some point, and this time will come, the repetitions of this cycle will lessen. Those same memories, songs, or things you see will begin to invoke a different response. It may cause you to smile rather than break with pain. It may cause you to reflect rather than scream in anguish. The Holy Spirit will empower you to meet those same things with peace because the Comforter has given you strength. This may take days, weeks or months. However long it takes, let the Holy Spirit in, and allow Him to help you through this time.

Chapter 4

WHEN GOD SAYS NO

There will come a time in everyone's life when a prayer of faith will still be met with the answer no. You may have prayed for a loved one's healing that never came and still resulted in a seemingly untimely, unfair death. You may have prayed for the restoration of a marriage, yet your spouse still walked away and never looked back. Whatever your prayer, it was one offered in complete faith that the God you serve would hear. You stood on the scripture in John 14:13–14 (KJV), which says, "And whatsoever ye shall ask in my name, that will I do, that the Father may be glorified in the Son. If ye shall ask any thing in my name, I will do it." You believed this wholeheartedly. You called on the intercessors, the prayer warriors, your pastor, and those in the faith to touch and agree with you because you understand the Word of God also says in Matthew 18:19 (KJV), "Again I say unto you, That if two of you shall agree on earth as touching any thing that they shall ask, it shall be done for them of my Father which is in heaven." The prayers went up, and yet that loved one still died, that spouse still left, that dream you believed in was not realized, and you were left broken and empty.

In a moment not only have you been left grieving a devastating loss in your life, but you've also found yourself feeling like you have nowhere to turn and no one to turn to. The God you believed in seems light years away. If He did not answer the earnest prayer you offered on behalf of this situation, why would He answer now if you called? Where was He? Who do you turn to when the faith you held on to for so long seems to have failed you? Where do you go when you find yourself grieving what feels like both a natural *and* spiritual loss?

This is the time that you have to dig deep within the depths of yourself to acknowledge that what you currently feel has no bearing on the truths that you already *know*. Like the common cliché says, "The truth hurts." This is the time you must acknowledge that even in the middle of this unfair circumstance, God is still God. He's no less worthy of honor, respect, worship, and praise than He was before this occurred. He's the same God that said yes to so many prayers before. He's the same God that picked you up out of your mess and called you to salvation. He's still God—one that sees beyond today to a future you cannot begin to comprehend.

If you knew that the child you lost would suffer greatly during this life, would you find solace in knowing she went peacefully from the womb? If you knew the business you had would have been in the way of the greater opportunity had it succeeded, would you still feel like a failure or appreciate the new door God has for you just around the corner? Sometimes God's no spares us from what would be more unbearable. Other times, it serves a greater purpose that fulfills a kingdom plan.

Yet other times, the answer may be, "No—for now." The yes could be for an appointed time that has not yet come.

"For my thoughts are not your thoughts, neither are your ways my ways, saith the Lord. For as the heavens are higher than the earth, so are my ways higher than your ways, and my thoughts than your thoughts" (Isaiah 55:8–9 KJV). Even though you cannot understand why God's answer was no, you have to remind yourself of the truth stated in the above scripture. The truth hurts—but it also is a starting point for healing. You may never know the purpose for your pain, but you must remember that God's plan for your life reaches far beyond what you can see right now. Jeremiah 29:11 (NLT) says, "For I know the plans I have for you," says the Lord. "They are plans for good and not for disaster, to give you a hope and a future." Even in an empty place, be reminded and encouraged that, for you, the sun will shine again because that too is in the plan of God.

Chapter 5

FORWARD... BACKWARD... FORWARD

My husband plays this particular video game that I've grown quite fond of watching. The storyline follows three main characters that, in the beginning, don't seem to have much in common. As the game progresses, you see that their lives intertwine in ways you would never have been able to imagine in the beginning. During the game play, you see the main characters complete assignments that bring them closer to their ultimate goal, and then they suddenly suffer major setbacks that cause them to reassess how to proceed. They have to find new routes to get to their destinations and at times, come up with new game plans to complete their missions. They move forward, then sometimes it looks as if they have to go backward to get further ahead.

In life, sometimes a setback becomes a set-up for a major comeback! Setbacks, if met with the correct response, can become a catalyst to the greatest accomplishments in our lives. God can use those tests to create the greatest testimonies. In the beginning, that may not matter to you at all. That is because you'd give anything to reverse the tide and bring back the joy, peace, and calm you experienced before the raging storm hit. No one asks for rain while basking in the sun. Yet when the rain comes, you are given a choice—you can sulk and complain about it knowing that won't change the forecast—or you can grab the umbrella and keep moving while it's coming down. And if the winds are too strong for the umbrella, retreat (momentarily) until the gusts abate before venturing out again.

Sometimes moving forward requires a few steps backward to get to the next place in life. The interesting thing about moving in God is that your steps are already orchestrated and are a part of His plan for your life.

What seems like steps backward to *you* are actually progressive steps to God if you are walking in His will. Psalm 37:23 in The Message Bible says so beautifully: "Stalwart walks in step with God; his path blazed by God, he's happy. If he stumbles, he's not down for long; God has a grip on his hand." How wonderful to know that if you find yourself in an empty place, God is with you and will not allow you to remain there for long. He has a grip (a firm hold and a tight grasp) on your hand and will pull you back to a place of peace!

Chapter 6

DON'T DO THIS, DO THAT

Don't do this; do that. Many people will try to tell you how to handle what is occurring in your life right now. Some will have the advice you need at a time you don't want to hear it. However, there will come a time when you will need to assess how you are dealing with the tragedy you are facing to ensure you are headed toward healing. Evaluate yourself to make sure you are taking the appropriate steps in the right direction. All roads lead to somewhere—just not always to where you need to be. Make sure the road you are on is taking you down the right path.

Don't do this ...

Don't indulge in destructive behaviors. It may seem like your world has fallen apart and therefore nothing else matters—but it does! The decisions you make at this moment are critical and can push you farther down rather than aid in your ascension back to that place of peace. Don't revisit past, destructive relationships. They are over for a reason. Don't dabble in alcohol and drugs. That will only provide a momentary escape from the reality that still awaits you once the high wears off. If you are not ready to face that reality, you will find yourself repeating the cycle of chasing a high to keep you from dealing with the matter at hand. This opens the door to the spirit of addiction.

Don't isolate yourself. It is normal to want to be alone for a period of time when going through a devastating situation. But be mindful that there are people who care about you and want to be with you to help you through. Find someone who is willing to listen if you want to talk, or just sit with you if you find silence more comforting. Whatever you do, allow someone in before isolation becomes your new norm. This opens the door to the spirit of depression.

Don't cover your pain with positions or possessions. It is easier to hide beneath your work than to work through the healing process. It is equally easier to invest in things (possessions) rather than invest in dealing with what is going on within yourself. Both routes will prove unfruitful in the end. The world may see you as strong and people may shower you with accolades for handling your grief with such resolve, but inside you are wounded, broken, and bitter. Hurting people hurt people. If you cover your pain, you will eventually cause others pain.

Do this …

Talk it through with God first—and then with someone you trust. At some point, begin talking. Bring your feelings to God in prayer. If you have someone, talk to that person who is willing to listen without being judgmental. Your thoughts may seem to lack rationale or may even sound outrageous, but they are yours, and you are entitled to them. Most of all, God already knows what has been swimming continually through your mind. Get it all out so it doesn't continue to eat at you on the inside.

Find your way back. Before the disappointment, before the pain and devastation, you were happy. You can be that again, but you must begin taking steps to find your way back. Take moments to appreciate what still remains before you after this experience. You are alive—so *live*! As long as God woke you up this morning, you have another chance to *live*. Don't let what has happened rob you of the life you still have yet to live. I know it seems hard, but take baby steps. If you have to start just by telling God "thank you" for allowing you another day, then you have begun by acknowledging He is still there and the opportunity to live still remains.

Go to the temple. I would be remiss if I didn't direct you to the hospital. You have been severely wounded by life's circumstances. Trying to recover without the proper medical attention would be careless and detrimental to your long-term recovery. You must find yourself back in the house of God. If you've never been, this is the perfect time to go. The temple (the church) is the hospital, and Jesus is fully capable of providing complete restoration for your soul. The temple is where you are continually provided the appropriate course of antibiotics to heal the deepest hurts. This is where you go for your follow-up appointments and where, when you are discharged, you will have a clean bill of health. When He sends you out, you will have conviction for your witness, a clear testimony, and a newfound purpose in your pain.

Chapter 7

THERE'S PURPOSE IN YOUR PAIN

Purpose is the reason for which something is done or created or for which something exists. Pain is physical or mental suffering, distress, or torment. So, how can there be a reason for which one must endure physical, mental, and/or emotional suffering, distress, or torment? I could sit here and tell you that just knowing there is a purpose behind what you have had to endure will make it easier—but that would not be true.

We know that physical pain is a signal to the brain that something is wrong. Congenital analgesia is a dangerous medical condition where one *cannot* feel pain. People with this condition can develop unnoticed infections, fracture bones, and even get burned without feeling a thing. Naturally, they are not equipped with a signal to the brain that something is wrong. Imagine what life is like for them. Now find yourself thinking if you never knew something was wrong, would the opportunity arising to fix it come too late? Spiritually, pain is sometimes allowed so God can bring to light something detrimental that has been festering for too long.

Ask yourself—is there something in what you've endured that forced you to face something you have not wanted to deal with? Or has this experience revealed something in you that God has been trying to teach you but to no avail? We must get to the place where the pain we feel can be used to root out what needs to be fixed within. Pain is not designed to be comfortable. Instead it exposes. Pain reveals our bitterness. Pain reveals our pride. Pain reveals our feelings of rejection and even our waffling faith in God. These feelings are not products of our experience; they had a hidden presence that was exposed by our experience.

The purpose in our pain may begin with helping to uproot those things God desires to strip from us—but it does not end there. And if you will accept the *greater* purpose for your life, you will find peace in knowing God's plan for you is bigger than you could have imagined. In Ezekiel 24 we find that the mandate God had on Ezekiel's life cost him his very desire—his wife. The charge to be an example to a great nation of people was larger than the life of the one he loved. Ezekiel 24:15–24 (KJV) says:

> Also the word of the Lord came unto me, saying, Son of man, behold, I take away from thee the desire of thine eyes with a stroke: yet neither shalt thou mourn nor weep, neither shall thy tears run down. Forbear to cry, make no mourning for the dead, bind the tire of thine head upon thee, and put on thy shoes upon thy feet, and cover not thy lips, and eat not the bread of men. So I spake unto the people in the morning:

and at even my wife died; and I did in the morning as I was commanded. And the people said unto me, Wilt thou not tell us what these things are to us, that thou doest so? Then I answered them, The word of the Lord came unto me, saying, Speak unto the house of Israel, Thus saith the Lord God; Behold, I will profane my sanctuary, the excellency of your strength, the desire of your eyes, and that which your soul pitieth, and your sons and your daughters whom ye have left shall fall by the sword. And ye shall do as I have done: ye shall not cover your lips, nor eat the bread of men. And your tires shall be upon your heads, and your shoes upon your feet: ye shall not mourn nor weep; but ye shall pine away for your iniquities, and mourn one toward another. Thus Ezekiel is unto you a sign; according to all that he hath done shall ye

> do: and when this cometh, ye shall know
> that I am the Lord God.

God's plan is greater than our desires, and with that understanding, we can find purpose in the pain we are graced to endure. That may not be something you want to hear—but as we've learned, the truth hurts—but it can also set you free. God trusts you enough to face the biggest battles in your own life to help win the greatest wars for another!

A respected evangelist I know once said, "Your *yes* could cost you everything." Did not Christ's *yes* cost Him His very life? Jesus did not end His own suffering or change His own circumstances because that was not a part of God's plan for His life. We, as children of God, must learn that following God means sometimes losing what we hold dear to obtain what we long for most—eternity in heaven. This life we know will cease to exist at some point, and if we continue to focus on temporal things, we will miss that which is eternal.

FOUND IN EMPTINESS

Emptiness is the place where it seemed nothing could be found nor anything contained. You see, the empty place is always accepting guests. There's never a shortage of availability. However, I challenge you to take up residence at a different location. There is a place of fullness in God that may never come with all of the answers you seek, but I can assure you there is one amenity it does not lack—*peace.* It is my prayer that after reading this book, you can see in your emptiness you were never lost to God—He was always there with you. He was waiting for you to find Him. Now that you have, allow Him to lead you back to your destiny and your profound purpose for this life.

Father, I thank You for being with me in the darkest hours of my life. Thank You for never giving up on me.

I acknowledge that even though I could not see You, in my emptiness You were always there. It was You who brought me through by Your unfailing love and grace. And I know it will be You who will use what I have endured to propel me into the destiny You have designed for my life. I surrender this void to you. Fill me up, Lord, with Your presence, that I may never be empty again. My life I surrender for Your glory. In Jesus's name, amen.

www.ingramcontent.com/pod-product-compliance
Ingram Content Group UK Ltd.
Pitfield, Milton Keynes, MK11 3LW, UK
UKHW020230250726
13967UKWH00001B/280

9 781483 471631